Tales of a

Glasgow Childhood

Tales of a

Glasgow Childhood

by

Jenny Chaplin

Acknowledgement is due to KEN LAIRD, editor of 'SCOTTISH MEMORIES',* to the pages of which prestigious magazine, Jenny Chaplin is a frequent contributor.

*'SCOTTISH MEMORIES' is published by LANG SYNE PUBLISHERS Ltd, Unit 2B, The Clydeway Centre, 45 Finnieston Street, GLASGOW G3 8JU. Telephone 041-204 3104   Fax 041-204 3101.

Previous books by this author include:

ONE EDITOR'S LIFE *(Writers' Own Publications)*

* A GLASGOW FAIR

* A GLASGOW HOGMANAY

* A GLASGOW CHILDHOOD

* ADRIFT IN ROTHESAY

   * *All published by Premier Publications, Rothesay)*

THE PUZZLE OF PARKINSON'S DISEASE
                    (Writers' Rostrum Publications)

AS EDITOR:

FORMING A WRITERS' GROUP
                              (Stephen Loveless)
WRITERS' OMNIBUS
                              (Cyril Mountjoy)
THE DARK SIDE OF THE MOON
                              (Fay Goldie)
PUT WRITING FIRST
                              (Muriel Barnett)
TALES OUT OF SCHOOL
                    (Cifford/Boyle/Kinnon/Chaplin)

WRITERS' ROSTRUM ANTHOLOGIES

THOUGHTS ON WRITING
          (Fay Goldie/Valerie Cuthbert/Jenny Chaplin)

CONTENTS

Page

TALES OF A GLASGOW CHILDHOOD

Introduction

When I first put pen to paper to record 'TALES OF A GLASGOW CHILDHOOD', it suddenly struck me forcibly that what I would be writing would in fact be history! Born in 1928 into a 'single-end' - what today would be called a 'deprived' home - I lived through the Depression Years with their scourge of unemployment, misery and privation; and later faced the trauma of wartime evacuation when many of the evacuees from the 'hovels of Glasgow' were treated as nothing other than lower-caste scum.

But was it all gloom and doom? Far from it! There was the loving home - tiny though it decidedly was - but cosy with its gleaming black range and the soup-pot ever on the boil with bubbling lentil and ham ambrosia; there was the caring camaraderie of a tightly-knit community, the other families and neighbours who all lived 'up oor close'; there was the strict, yet unresented, discipline of the local Primary school, where we sat at wooden benches, the latter arranged in tiered platforms. At all times, we sat bolt upright with arms folded, as we hung on teacher's every word, aye ready to jump at the word of command, lest her Lochgelly belt would come crashing down on our chilblained hands; and of course, there was the utter joy of Saturday matinees at the local 'flea-pit' where for a carefully-hoarded tuppence we could escape for a few hours at least, the hell-hole that was Glasgow in the Thirties and gallop off into the Hollywood sunset with Hopalong Cassidy and his trusty steed.

And what of the 'characters', those kenspeckle figures who were an integral part of my childhood and whose presence, antics and often total eccentricity added a certain zest to our 'deprived' lives? There was Granny McGuinness, immediate neighbour, holy terror of small children and 'Queen O' Ra Close'; Auld Leerie, the lamplighter with his wee 'bandy' legs and long gas-lighting pole; 'Stinkey Malinkey', the fish-wife with her sack-cloth apron, man's 'bunnet' and her raucous voice which, together with a blast from her brass bugle, would awaken the dead, far less the sleeping unemployed of Govan; and we mustn't forget the 'Wee Insurance Man' who collected the penny-a-week towards your 'Funeral Fund'; the coal-briquette hawker; the 'Ticky Man'; the ragman with his promises of untold - and usually unproduced - riches; the usherette with her impressive uniform and her torch, a badge of office which somehow bestowed on her the absolute power to chuck us weans 'oota ra local flea-pit', should we ever dare to become rather too unruly; the knife-grinder on his bicycle; and the Terror of our lives - a mythical being who went by the name of Flannel-Feet, a creature of the night whom none of us weans had actually ever seen, but whose spectre and very name haunted the after-dark streets and terrorised our vivid imaginations. Yes! Characters one and all and now part of Glasgow's history.

There were visits on the tramcar to see Granny Brigton who lived in the East End of the City; family outings to such famous Glasgow landmarks as the Kelvingrove Art Galleries and in the posh, 'toffee-nosed' West End, to the Botanic Gardens with the world-famous green-houses; the 'Barras' where we shopped for bargains, not forgetting 'Paddy's Market' under the railway arches; Sunday-school trips, when complete with enamel mug strung around the neck, we would 'jour-ney', or otherwise march in an orderly 'crocodile' to the Fifty Pitches', there to run races and eat a cold Scotch mutton-pie and a fern cake; Highland Dancing at Glasgow Green...

There was the annual thrill of 'Ra Glesga Ferr', Glas-gow's somewhat Bacchanalian exodus from the 'Second City of the Empire', when sick with excitement, we would travel by Clyde steamer a few miles 'doon ra watter'  to Rothesay, 'The Madeira of Scotland'; then Hallowe'en, when suitably disguised in a few borrowed rags, we could wander the mean, ill-lit City streets without fear of harassment; and of course, the grand finale to the year, Hogmanay, when no matter what hellish trauma we or our relatives, friends and neighbours had endured throughout the previous twelve months, we would nevertheless celebrate in memorable fashion, do our 'party-pieces' and toast the New Year and whatever it would bring in its wake, in a spirit of hope and anticipation, all washed down with a plentiful libation of Granny McGuinness's ginger-wine for the weans, and for the adults, the even more potent and enjoyable libation of not a few hefty tots of Teacher's best whisky, obviously the 'water of life.'

But there is more, much more to tell - so why not join me on a journey down memory lane, as we take a fond look at a bygone age in 'TALES OF A GLASGOW CHILDHOOD.'

FOOD FOR THOUGHT

In the days of Glasgow Depression
when fear filled our lives,
did we live in terror of
muggings and slashings,
drug-crazed louts and terrorist reprisals,
air-raids and nuclear attack,
airplane crashes and motorway pile-ups,
mortgage repayments and devaluation of the pound,
global warming and holes in the ozone layer,
Third World disaster and
over-population of the Planet Earth,
redundancy?
No!
Our only fear
was that of unemployment
with its legacy
of poverty, depression
and misery.

THE DEATH-KNELL FOR GOVAN

In the years of the Depression, and during all the time that my brother and I were growing up in Govan, the scourge of unemployment was spreading its tentacles of cancer throughout Britain, and certainly not least in Glasgow.

The Shipyards of my own immediate neighbourhood - FAIRFIELDS, STEPHENS OF LINTHOUSE, HARLAND and WOLFF of Govan, all of them proud, skilled and highly efficient builders of fine ocean-going vessels, now stood bleak and empty, deserted as they were of all human life and activity. When the Depression was at its lowest ebb, the only inhabitants of the formerly bustling Shipyards were the scuttling rats and the empty stocks, with their skeletal rib-cages, which resembled nothing so much as tenement-high, prehistoric monsters.

And what of the men, the previous workforce, who had taken such a pride in their hard-won skills of joinery, riveting, baulking and draughtsmanship... shipbuilders one and all.

With nothing in the way of paid employment and all day in which to do it, groups of such dispirited men were to be found on every street corner, huddled together as though for mutual support in their ongoing misery. Their 'uniform' was a thin suit, long white tasselled scarf, and their badge of office, a flat tweed 'bunnet'. Each man wore his 'bunnet' straight on his head with the skip pulled low over his forehead. And with the canny, inborn instinct of the slum child, I always knew better than to disturb those men. True, there would be neighbours lurking under those 'bunnets', but I had no right to look into their eyes, eyes in which would doubtless be mirrored the hopelessness, the misery, but above all the shame and the unsought guilt of unemployment. No! instinctively I knew it was far better to leave these poor souls to whatever peace they could find, for under such shelter could be seen no poverty, no empty Shipyards, no rat-infested tenements and no shawl-clad women grown old before their time with the double burden of too many weans and never enough siller for essential food with which to fill their empty bellies.

To a man, their hands were inevitably thrust deep into the pockets of those hand-me-down suits. The only movement was the shuffling of ill-shod feet, as they trailed back and forward from one street corner to the next. Their vain hope was that such pointless meandering would not only defeat the intense cold, but at the same time, in some magical way, transport them beyond the mean, litter-strewn streets of Govan to a better life, where there would be work, dignity and money enough for all... a Shangri-la, far removed from the misery and degradation which was then the sum total of their lives.

My Father was luckier than most other Govanites in that he had an alternative form of employment ready to hand. His Father, who rejoiced in the name of 'Auld Mac', owned a small business in Elder Street and the very moment that the shadow of unemployment fell on our own little household, then my Grandfather at once offered to accept my Father as a trainee cook. The only rather daunting problem to this arrangement was that Grandfather's business was that of a self-styled 'WORKMEN'S RESTAURANT'. And the obvious problem was that with now only a handful, or even no workmen at all, to come streaming round the corner from Fairfields, in search of a hot meal at mid-day, the Restaurant itself now lay as silent and as deserted as the Govan Shipyards themselves. At least it was still open and that in stark contrast to the dozens of other shops with paint-peeling facades, whose appearance did nothing to relieve the gloom that was Govan in the early Nineteen-Thirties.

It is worth pointing out that at this stage in its history, Auld Mac's WORKMEN'S RESTAURANT had already been a long-established and successful institution in Govan for close on twenty years. But now the previously thriving village which had been Govan, had ground to an uneasy halt with the demise of the Shipyards and their ancillary trades - it was almost as if

6

Govan was stuck fast in a time-warp of gloom, poverty and despondency. So what was to be done?

Well, my Grandfather, never one to give up easily, and realising full well that although he personally could do nothing about the major problem of the deserted Shipyards, nevertheless, there was something he could do to alleviate our own immediate family's desperate financial worries. With two families now to be fed, clothed and housed from the ever-dwindling profits, he suddenly came up with a bright idea... he and my Dad would put their heads together and come up with something, anything which might bring about sweeping changes in the business and hopefully bring some money into the too-empty shop-till. Mention of the latter reminds that even this essential object - a far cry from the modern sophisticated, computerised tills of today - would by now be in itself something of a museum piece! In effect, it was nothing other than a pull-out drawer, the interior of which boasted a stout wooden frame, parts of which had been hollowed out by some skilful local carpenter to form smooth, deep recesses for the different values of coinage. As I recall, the smallest bowl was reserved for the tiny silver threepenny-bits, with the next in size being kept for farthings. An astute businessman in later life, Grandfather also had nailed to the broad rim of the drawer a number of foreign and otherwise 'dud' coins, which although at first and casual glance appeared to be a 'good likeness', nevertheless were NOT coins of the Realm! Legend had it that as a young and 'makkee-learn' shopkeeper, Grandfather had been duped by the said coins, forever nailed to the till. Not that he himself would ever admit to such a thing, but nonetheless, it must be said that he always made a point of initiating in the ways of high finance any new or inexperienced helpers he took on. Thus, even as a not-very-streetwise wee lassie, I could still spot a dud sixpence or an immigrant foreign coin at a mile off!

My Grandfather had been 'deid richt' when he had opined that he and my Father were both 'bloody lucky' to have jobs of any kind at that time, for those last dying notes of the Shipyard work-hooters had indeed sounded the death-knell for the previously industrious district of Govan and its now utterly wretched inhabitants.

On the other hand, what good was a job with no money attached to it and little by way of legal currency coming into the till? Something had to be done and done quickly for the salvation of our little family... but what? Grandfather and my Dad were both agreed that no matter whether men were employed in the yards or merely existing on the pittance of the Dole, the one fact remained - they and their families would still have to eat, wouldn't they? So, instead of waiting meekly for the 'workers' to come in for a 'sit-doon' meal, as had been the case in the happy days of full employment, why not instead organise a 'carry-oot' operation? That way, the hard-pressed womenfolk of the unemployed could come in and get, at a reasonable cost and at no extra trouble to themselves - a bowl of steaming-hot mince and tatties or a jug of delicious home-made Scotch broth. Brilliant!

Once they had inaugurated the 'carry-oot' trade, business began to improve. But even so, there was still barely enough money to support the needs of two families. Something else would need to be done, and quickly at that! It was then decided - they would advertise! And so at the tender age of eight years, I was conscripted to the advertising executive board, my first remit being that of writing up a few words, preferably in verse, such as would later entice people to come along with their plates, bowls, jugs - and money - to sample our delicious wares of mince and tatties, mutton and ashet pies and Scotch broth. Perhaps this assignment was the start of my career as a writer? Who knows! What is sure is that after many pencil-chewing hours, at the end of which I was no nearer completing my task, I cast around for inspiration. It was then that my eyes alighted on our long-established 'gimmick', the three pottery pigs who had stood in the shop-window for as long as I could remember. Where Grandfather had first bought the pigs I was never sure, but whatever their origin, they were, and always had been, an integral part of my childhood. About a foot high, each pig stood tall and proud on two little trotters while the other two trotters had been fashioned to hold the rods which in turn held the trays of my Father's delicious apple tarts and Scotch mutton pies. One pig, obviously the boss, wore a checked waistcoat and a gaffer's bowler hat, while the other two sported long white aprons, such as my Father also wore for his work. Inspiration found at long last, I penned my first-ever poem in the white-heat of enthusiasm, thus launching into the high-flown realms of literature! Judge for yourself!

'Three little pigs
in the window are we...
And what do we eat
Every day for our tea?
Mac's pies and Scotch broth
make us big and strong;
So get your Mammy
to bring YOU along...

AND

Come to Auld Mac's
for soup and snacks.'

True to his promise of publication, Grandfather contacted a local printer who produced my work-of-art on leaflets, which I then had the doubtful pleasure of delivering through hundreds of letter-boxes in our immediate neighbourhood. For weeks after, I trailed up and down gas-lit, crumbling tenement stairs, delivering this poignant advert and my first published work. Perhaps I should point out here that my love-affair with the written word started with that far-distant, but never forgotten, first 'Editorial acceptance.'

But proud as I was of my first published literary effort, even I knew that no childish words of mine could ever have done full justice to the steaming pots of soup that Grandpa and my dear Dad made day after weary day. It is only with hindsight and the writing experience of fifty years that I can now say:

'Oh! But it was good that soup! With stewing beef at tuppence the pound and a cornucopia of vegetables, it was a wonder there was a carrot or a turnip left in any field within ten miles of Govan. Long before the hour of Noon, the women in their ragged shawls, and children, all knees and elbows in their dark Parish jerseys, would push their way forward in the queue, each pressing for a glimpse, a smell of the steaming, delicious brew. My Dad would preside over the cauldron and with each stir, each tuppeny-worth poured into each waiting, chipped enamel jug, those further back in the line would be in an agony of indecision. Might the day's supply of soup run out before it was their turn; or on the other hand, was it better to hang back in the hope that they would get the last serving with the rich scrapings of any vegetables which were still sticking to the bottom of the pot?'

One of the proudest days of my life was when Dad, pleased with the success of my 'poem', allowed me the singular honour of choosing the colour of the gaffer-pig's shirt for the ensuing year. The Nobel prize for Literature was as nothing compared to that unique honour! The thing was that both Grandpa and Dad, knowing full well what a 'draw' were the three little pigs, each Spring, as soon as the first daffodil appeared in our local Elder Park, they would give the pigs their annual refit. Then, once more spruced up and cleaned and repainted, they would

THREE LITTLE PIGS

IN THE WINDOW ARE WE

again take up their stance in our shop window. Half a century ago, people had never heard of 'gimmicks' and other such advertising inducements to part them from their money, so with our resident 'attraction', Auld Mac's window soon became something of a nine-days wonder. People on the Dole, starved not only of essential food, but also of anything in the way of free entertainment or any such light relief from the drab greyness of their humdrum daily lives, began to flock from miles around to see the 'famous' pigs in the window of Auld Mac's Workmen's Restaurant.

If our harmless advertising 'gimmick' and our three little pigs brought at least a glimmer of a smile and a moment of happiness to those poor, downtrodden and dispirited unemployed folk, then I am glad... for God help them, they needed all the light relief they could get... life on the Dole in Glasgow during the harrowing years of the Depression was no joke, either for the men themselves or their poor, overworked wives and their ragged, barefoot weans. That indeed was the reality of life on Glasgow's Clydeside during those terrible, soul-destroying years... years which should never be forgotten but which should be given their rightful - if unhappy - place in the history books for the benefit of future generations. And hopefully, in this way, the misery of their tortured lives will not have been in vain.

MAMMY KNEW BEST -
BUT AH WAS JIST NAE LADY

Like many another bairn whose mammy was hell-bent on her off-spring 'getting on in life', from an early age - and at great financial hardship to my parents - I was sent to self-improvement classes. In my case, these fell into three categories - dancing classes, elocution lessons and piano tuition.

As far as the dancing classes went, by the time I was six years old, I could do a Heilan Fling, a Sword Dance, an Irish washerwoman, or an aproned, be-clogged little Dutch girl routine with the best of them. Then there was Tap-dancing, when with steel plates affixed to an old pair of school-shoes which my father had painted red for the occasion, I tap-toed my way towards the bright hope of becoming another Shirley Temple! When that dream faded, Mammy decided that with my 'moosey-broon' hair perhaps I was rather more of a 'Highland Dancer'. So from that moment on, that would become my forte.

I was then kitted out in the best Highland outfit which money and the 'Ticky-man' could provide. To this day, I've never known if Mammy's choice of tartan was a conscious decision, or whether it just happened to be the only suitably-priced one available in my size at the time!

Anyhow, I was soon decked out in a kilt of the dress MacMillan tartan. With its brilliant red and yellow checks, matching top-hose, red velvet jacket and all the other essential accoutrements such as tartan plaid, lace jabot, brooch and 'silver' buckles on my shin, I felt that I stood out like 'a sair thumb.'

To my child's eye, at least, it seemed that all the other dance competitors were dressed in rather more sombre hues, while yours truly was the unwilling and weepy rainbow in their midst.

Self-conscious or not, I went with Mammy to as many Highland Dance Competitions as we could afford and in this way, travelled 'doon the watter' to such venues as Rothesay, Dunoon and Greenock, as well as to Glasgow Green and many Town Halls.

In due time, my chest was covered with an assortment of cheap medals, which if anything, clanking away like a busy day on the Clyde shipyards, only added to my embarrassment ... shrinking violet that I was!

And of course, in order to keep up to the mark of Competition standard, and with the constant hopes of my winning a Silver Cup or some other such prestigious Trophy, I had to attend my weekly dancing classes. My teacher was a beautiful blonde lady, a Mrs. Wright, and as far as I can remember at this distance in time, our classes were held at various draughty halls in the Govan and the Linthouse areas of Glasgow.

The high spot of our hours, weeks and long months of practice was our annual Display which was held in South Govan Town Hall. Young as I was, I often felt that as far as our annual Display went, there was more drama behind the scenes than ever made it to the footlights! I can see it yet ... ambitious mothers hovering around weeping, over-excited weans, and our 'cheer-leader' diving about with a worried frown on her face and in her hands a box of safety-pins at the ready for those times when, at the crucial moment, some poor wee wean's knicker-elastic gave up the unequal struggle!

However, I can well remember one occasion when there was a dramatic and totally unrehearsed incident on stage.

I must have been about six at the time and with pointed cap and crudely made set of large ears, I was done up to look like nobody's idea of an elf. Our remit and well-rehearsed routine had led us to the point where we had to skip through the 'forest' at dead of night, then hide behind a 'tree'. The idea was that when the star-spangled Fairy Queen gallumphed on to the stage, she would be quizzed as to the possible whereabouts of her mischievous band of elfin-helpers. Okay! So far, so good, everything going to plan when suddenly up the steps at the front of the stage clambered a single-minded and very determined member of the audience! Now the Fairy Queen really did have a wee bit of a problem - who was the interloper and what was the purpose of the interruption?

It turned out to be none other than ma wee cousin Maggie, who at the tender and totally uninhibited age of three years, had just seen her favourite playmate disappear behind a tree up on a brightly-lit stage. Determined to investigate and greet me in her usual fashion of a big sloppy kiss, the sturdy toddler marched over to the tree and started dragging out her bashful and black-affrontit cousin into the limelight. That done, she started slobbering me with kisses, to the utter amazement of the Fairy Queen, who at this change in our set-routine, looked decidedly 'pit-oot', as if some wee nyaff had just 'stole her sody-scone'. As for the by-now delighted onlookers in the audience, they collapsed in gales of helpless, tears-runnin'-doon-the-cheeks laughter. I sometimes felt that that infamous occasion was the nadir of my dancing career!

Like so many hard-working, well-meaning, under-nourished and impoverished Scottish mothers of the Thirties era, Mammy felt that it would be ill-afforded money well-spent for lessons on elocution. Equating the possession of a refined English accent with good breeding and all the finer things of life Mammy sought out a genteel lady. This grande-dame with a pseudo-English accent and the condescension of a minor Royal, let it be known that she would unbend sufficiently, to 'take in' (and this doyen of high society never said a truer word!) 'take in a few, very select group of private pupils.'

Not only had I to learn to speak 'Posh' with a damned great bool in ma mooth, I was also expected to learn by heart, reams of the most pan-loaf and sick-making poetry. Even today I can remember one Poetry Reading Competition when about fifty or more well-primed contestants from all over Glasgow gathered in a hall in the West End of the city. Well, let's face it, it would have to be the West End, wouldn't it ... the home of the Kelvinside accent and a place where everybody spoke 'proper.'

We each had a set piece to deliver, and that only after taking up the appropriate stance of feet together and hands cupped decorously in the manner of some would-be Prima Donna. So there I was, as prissy and toffee-nosed as the rest, as I launched into the poet's memorable words which followed the mind-blowing title of - wait for it -

"A Duck, A Duck, the Story of A Duck."

By the time the captive audience of parents, grannies, granpas, aunties and uncles had heard the same poem for about the fortieth time, there were dark rumblings and much rustling of sweetie-pokes to be heard from the main body of the hall. Even worse, especially for yours truly who thought that she had recognised Granpa Mac's voice, gradually being bandied about were some well-known Glesca words and phrases which appeared to rhyme with the word 'Duck.'

Having lost her battle in the matter of accents, Mammy still had one shot in the locker - it would be a very 'refeened' thing for her daughter to learn to play the piano. So, an excellent teacher was soon found - a maiden lady of indeterminate age who lived in a little terrace house opposite Govan's Pirrie Park. Miss Brown, a stickler for discipline, had hands as icy as a long-deid corpse ... and a sense of humour to match!

I'll spare you the gory details of the many tearful scenes endured, as I struggled against impossible odds to master the ivories, and then struggled even harder to wangle myself out of the essential music practice on our newly-bought and heavily-mortgaged Thompson's piano. I used all my childish wiles to get out of playing that damned piano, so that I could join my pals for such street games as 'Leavo/Peever/Skipping/and Kick the Can.'

As might have been expected, the pull of the street-games and the company of ma pals was much too strong. That being the case ... yes! You've got it in one! I did not make it as a concert pianist!

But at least in the years that followed, I was able with some measure of expertise, to belt out reams of military-style music for generations of school-weans, as they marched into their Corporation Schools ... but that is another story altogether, and one which I'll save for a future book of reminiscence.

A VISIT TO GRANNY BRIGTON

As a Scottish wean in the Glasgow of the Depression Years, one of my greatest 'treats' - and now one of my fondest memories - was to be taken on a visit to my maternal Granny who lived in the East End of the City. My wee bree, Telfie, and I always referred to her as 'Granny Brigton', and it was in a rare old state of excitement that we used to board the 'yella caur' in Govan for our journey.

Invariably Mammy would let us clamber to the top deck where, of course, we made a bee-line for the 'wee house' which was situated right above the tram driver's head. Then with the sliding door secured and the workaday world shut out, we would sit back in splendid isolation and enjoy the passing show. As the tramcar rattled along, we looked down on the rusting derricks, and deserted ship yards, the great warehouses, and the street after street of grey tenements, each with their quota of pubs and their 'Jenny-a-things' wee corner shops.

But for me, each time I travelled that route, the best sight of all was my first glimpse of Templeton's Carpet Factory. One of the biggest in the world, and certainly the biggest carpet factory in Britain, this building had a magic all its own. After the rows of drab, grey and crumbling tenements, Templeton's Carpet Factory stood out like a fairy-castle. 'Granny Brigton' had told us that the huge building had been built in the style of the Doge's Palace in Venice. Not that I'd have known Doge's Palace even if I'd seen it in my parraitch, but somehow, for me at least, the puzzling nugget of information only added to the building's fascination.

Not only that, but Granny had once told us in a very serious tone of voice, that if ever we passed the magnificent building on All Saints' Day, then we should say a prayer for the Faithful Departed, the poor souls of the Templeton workers who lost their lives in the calamity of November 1st, 1889...

Like many old people, Granny Brigton not only dwelt in the past, but she had total recall of long-gone events and would happily tell and re-tell the same stories to anyone patient enough to listen. I can hear

16

her yet -

"What with it being All Saints' Day, I'll never forget the date - and a real dull November day it was too. Just a young bride I was at the time and with your Grampa having found no work in Glasgow - that's right, notices everywhere stating that 'NO IRISH NEED APPLY', well, I was doing a spot o' cleaning for a grand lady round in Monteith Row. Yes! real swanky houses in the Row, that's where the gentry lived, the posh folk, ye know. Anyway, must have been about tea-time, the wind screaming outside, fair shaking the trees on the Green, I can tell you. Well, suddenly, there was this terrible noise - like a clap o' thunder, only worse. Some o' the menfolk in the house-hold ran outside to see what on earth had happened. It seemed that there had been a terrible accident - the mill had collapsed in the gale - the walls just caved in, trapping many of the girls and women. Yes! A real tragedy. More than fifty people lost their lives that night. Aye! A sad, sad business."

Later research on my part revealed that Granny's memory recall of the tragedy had been pretty accurate... The Evening Times of 2nd November, 1889 stated that '51 persons have lost their lives by the sad calamity and about 20 have received injuries.' Some of the workers were allowed home after on-the-spot medical attention, but those seri-ously injured were taken to Glasgow's Royal Infirmary.

Granny was wrong, however, in thinking that it was the actual mill itself which had crashed in on top of the workers. The building which did collapse in the North-west gale, was at the moment of im-pact, little more than a roofless shell, being still in the course of con-struction. It had been designed by Mr. William Leiper (1839-1916) an architect from Helensburgh who had previously built a number of fine churches such as Dowanhill and Hyndland in Glasgow's West End.

The new building was required to meet the demands of the grow-ing business and on completion, was intended to be a free-standing addition to the old weaving-sheds, then working to full capacity.

It seems that when originally Messrs. Templeton had indicated that they wanted to erect a large building facing on to Glasgow Green, they were told by the City Fathers, in no uncertain terms, that any building in such a situation 'must present a pleasing appearance.'

When after several proposed designs by lesser architects had been rejected by the City Fathers, this was when the shy bachelor, William Leiper was called to the scene. Messrs. Templeton, no doubt by then somewhat frustrated, got straight to the point and asked him what, in his opinion, was "the most beautiful building in the world?" He opted for "The Doge's Palace in Venice".

His remit then was to design something 'along the lines of The Doge's Palace'. This he did, and in due time, his plans were approved for a 60 ft broad and 200 ft long building, which would adequately house Templeton's manufacture of a new carpet fabric, patent rights for which had recently been acquired from an American inventor.

When the shell of the new building crashed down in the gale, it collapsed through the roof of the weaving-shed of the old mill, where close on 150 women and girls were working at 140 looms.

One can imagine the panic which followed as those lucky enough to be uninjured by the falling masonry rushed to escape. About 70 of the girls managed to make their way out to the safety of William Street, while some other brave souls stayed behind to comfort and offer what assistance they could to those of their friends and workmates who lay trapped beneath piles of bricks and rubble.

By now, the weaving-sheds had been plunged into total darkness and it was in these terrible conditions that the trapped and dying lay for upwards of two hours, as rescuers tore at the debris with bare hands in a desperate bid to rescue them.

An eye-witness later told an Evening Times reporter than when the Fire Brigade and the Salvage Corps arrived, by the flickering light of lamps and lanterns, 'they lent every assistance in the work of rescue.'

And at least one woman who was dragged only just alive from the wreckage, said that her rescuers had kept up her spirits by handing her in drinks of water and by frequent calls of:
'Cheer up, Lassie, we'll be sure to get you out.'

Rightly or wrongly, Granny Brigton always averred that the people of Glasgow forgot all too quickly about the poor unfortunates who died or were badly maimed in this calamity. Her theory was that since rebuilding started almost immediately, and with the completed structure itself being such a nine-days wonder, it was a case of 'out of sight, out of mind,' as far as the disaster victims and their bereaved and grieving families were concerned.

Hence her instruction to us weans always on All Saints' Day to 'say a wee prayer' for the Faithful Departed of the Templeton's Carpet Factory Calamity.

'SEE THON EVACUEES!'

Long before the outbreak of World War Two, plans for the evacuation of school-children from Glasgow had been organised. In March 1939, a notice was sent out from Mr R M Allardyce, Glasgow's Chief Education Officer.

Addressed to 'The Parents or Guardians of Children in Glasgow', and sub-headed: 'Evacuation of Children from Glasgow in the Event of a National Emergency', the form stated the exact plans which had been made. Parents were asked to consider whether their children should be included in the arrangements for the crowded areas of large cities, whereby children would be transferred to 'safer places if war should ever break out.' Further, they were advised that 'the children would gather at the Primary School nearest their home and the older and younger members of each family would as far as possible be evacuated together. They would go to the chosen places in the care of their teachers who would remain with them. They would live in the country in houses where they would be welcome.'

The actual evacuation started on September 1, 1939...

Wartime evacuation of children was a traumatic event for all concerned, Mammies, Daddies, Grannies, Grampas, Aunties, Uncles and not least, of course, for the City weans themselves. My wee bree and I were two such unsophisticated Glesga keelies who were assembled with our school pals, labelled like so many parcels and then shipped off to an unknown destination to houses either at the seaside or in the country, strange houses, where according to Glasgow's Education Officer, Allardyce, we 'would be welcome'.

With our cardboard-boxed gas-masks slung across one shoulder and across the other, a bulging school-bag from which peeped out spare pairs of navy school knickers and the essential Liberty Bodice, we must indeed have presented a pitiful sight.

As we marched along in military-style crocodile, we were all too aware of the luggage-label tied around our necks and the enamel mug on a string which dangled nonchalantly somewhere between the gasmask container and the school-bag. We were taken from Glasgow's Govan by bus to a ferry terminal somewhere down the Clyde coast, where in a rare old state of excitement, we boarded a boat for the next stage of our journey.

Most of our school-mates had never before been out of Glasgow in their young lives, far less travelled on a boat. In that respect at least, my wee bree, Telfie, and I were luckier than our companions. We were already experienced travellers, having been 'doon the watter' the previous summer on a never-to-be-forgotten holiday to Rothesay. Of course, even we realised that there was a vast difference between a holiday sail on a Clyde steamer when the ship had been brightly paint-ed, dressed overall with flags and bunting which waved in time to the ship's band; and a wartime boat painted battleship grey and with not so much as a German Band or even a destination board in sight.

Nobody thought to tell us where we were going - it was wartime after all, and it had already been instilled into us that 'careless talk cost lives', so we knew better than to ask any questions. So as we sailed across the Firth of Clyde that night, we had no idea as to what would be our eventual fate or even where we might lay our weary heads that bedtime.

As is often the way in such situations, rumour was rife. And no doubt aided by the vivid imaginations of some of the big girls and 'Qualy boys', we younger weans were soon in a panic - totally con-vinced that we were being kidnapped by 'thae durty Germans' and never again would we see Mammy, Daddy nor Glasgow again.

I remember it vividly ... all the port-holes had been boarded over, we could see nothing beyond the saloon into which we were herded and the grey-painted ship was grim and unwelcoming. And as if all that were not enough, add a rough crossing with scores of tearful children being sea-sick, as well as already homesick for the familiar and now far-away streets of Govan; scared out of their wits at the thought of the rumoured goose-stepping Germans now supposedly marauding the decks above our heads ... take all these things together and you get a clear picture of our situation.

Apart from our own teachers, our minders included a motley crew of young students, clerks and Sunday school-teachers who had been pressed into service in this emergency. They were having their own not inconsiderable problems in trying to cope efficiently with a mixed load of fractious and terrified evacuees. .

Years later in my world travels, I experienced some pretty horrendous mid-winter voyages in the Bay of Biscay but even they were a joy compared to that evacuation trip.

If we had thought the voyage was bad, even worse awaited us once we were safely ashore. No, it was not the Germans of our imagination who turned out to be the enemy - but rather the well-meaning officious ladies and gentlemen, the 'high heid yins' otherwise designated as our Billeting Officers. Their first remit was to herd us all into a draughty church hall, there to await the next step in processing us from City weans to bona-fide Clyde-coast evacuees.

Young as I was, it soon became clear to me that the high heid brain who had master-minded the operation, had obviously equated material poverty and a working-class district in Glasgow with filth, vermin and neglect. So, following this line of thinking, it was deemed essential that before we could be allocated to our host homes where we could be 'welcome', we must first be de-loused.

On all sides, I could see terrified small boys having their heads shaved and being left with an obscene tuft of hair sticking up at the front. As for the girls, they did fare a little better in that they were being given pudding-basin haircuts and the compensation of a can-can fringe.

I felt sick as I watched this operation. Not only that, I felt dirty, degraded and finally, very angry. Was it for this that Mammy had spent Daddy's hard-earned money on Derbac soap and the special steel-comb with which she industriously searched our hair for nits and other such live-stock every Friday night?

Fortunately, Telfie and I were at the end of the queue and as the shearers approached, wild thoughts went racing through my brain. Finally, when escape seemed impossible, I decided on a spot of positive action. Taking a firmer grip on my brother's hand, I bent down to his level, then whispered a few words in his ear. As I recall, it was a somewhat garbled message all about horrible giants, 'thae durty Germans' and their shears with which they would cut us both up into little pieces and throw us to the sharks in the river!

Whatever my hastily whispered words meant to Telfie, I'll never know, but they must have helped him to conjure up some pretty weird mental picture in his tiny mind. Anyway, the end result was that we both yelled, screamed, scratched and kicked to such good effect that eventually we were left to our own devices ... and still in proud possession of full blown head of hair apiece. Telfie's golden waves and curls still bounced across his now tear-begrutten face; while my crop of beribboned sausage-ringlets must have stood out as an affront to the unnecessary carnage scattered around us.

When my parents got word of the treatment we were being accorded, they at once made arrangements to have us repatriated to Glasgow and the lesser evils of the air-raids and the German bombs.

Not long after we arrived home, a bomb did drop on the nearby Benburb's Football Ground and blew out the windows of our new council house in Drumoyne, into which we had moved not long before. But apart from that near-miss and a period of uneventful private evacuation with a farmer's wife in Lanarkshire, my wee bree and I survived the rest of the war without incident.

For all that, the scars remained, only mental scars it is true, but very real for all that. In fact, it would be many years into adulthood before I could bear to hear the name 'Arran'; far less visit the village of Corrie on that beautiful Island ... the Island of our humiliation and shame.

Nowadays in retirement from a lifetime of teaching, I often give talks to Rotary, Writers' Circles, Women's Guilds and the like. After one such talk in the course of which I touched on my wartime evacuation experiences, I later had to deal with some rather irate ladies, who, it turned out had done their bit for the war effort as ... yes, you've guessed it ... Billeting Officers! I made no attempt to placate these war heroines but could only reiterate that I had not made up the story off the top of my head (if you'll forgive the pun) but that every word was true and I had simply told it 'the way it was.'

Further to that, I had since made a detailed study of newspapers of the period and found that apart from being labelled as 'dirty and verminous', many evacuees were discriminated against and in a great many ways.

Local newspapers of the time carried such banner headlines as: 'GLASGOW EVACUEE ABSCONDS'; 'MORE MISDEEDS BY EVACUEES' ... the latter relating to the fact that a householder, taken to court for having broken the Blackout regulation, blamed it all on the in-house evacuee! That, and many other 'crimes' too numerous to mention were laid at the door of the much maligned evacuees.

No doubt there were some children who did land in homes where they received the promised 'welcome'. They were the lucky ones who now have happy memories of a war spent at the Clyde resorts or in the Scottish countryside.

One strange anomaly is that as fast as Glesga weans were being hastily dumped at such seaside places as Bute, Millport, Dunoon, Arran and inland countryside locations such as Biggar and Coulter, there was a steady stream of local children who were being privately evacuated to Canada, America and South Africa. And at least one 'sea-vac' from Rothesay to Capetown wrote back in glowing terms of her new life in the sunshine of Africa where, she hastened to assure her parents, not only was she being well-treated, but she and her equally happy companions were always referred to not as 'sea-vacs', evacuees or any other derogatory term, but rather as 'our guest children'.

On the other hand, many children had a horrendous time in even trying to reach their new adoptive homes abroad. Take the case of the evacuee children from the Dutch liner 'VOLENDAM'. Due to the strict censorship restrictions of wartime, the attack on the 'VOLENDAM' was reported thus in a number of British newspapers on Friday 6, September, 1940:

Children's Liner Saved
-Towed into North British Port

'After a strenuous journey, four tugs have successfully towed into a North British port the liner which was torpedoed while carrying 320 school-children to Canada. The evacuee ship was torpedoed by a U-boat in the Atlantic, but not a single child was lost'.

Of the total 320 children aboard, 74 of them were Scottish. The miracle was that all the passengers were rescued and brought safely ashore to Greenock on the Clyde, the 'North British port' mentioned in the newspaper article. They arrived on the first day of September.

Clearly shaken from their ordeal and wearing carpet slippers and blanket-shawls, or in some cases school trench-coats to which were still attached somewhat crumpled identification labels, they were a sorry sight. But even so, the important thing was that they have been saved from a watery grave. And amazingly, some of the younger girls had managed to rescue favourite, if rather damp, baby dolls.

Two weeks later, these same survivor children, now rested and apparently none the worse for their ordeal, apart from their inner mental scars, were re-shipped for yet another stab at evacuation across the Atlantic to America or Canada.

This time they sailed out of Liverpool in the 'CITY OF BE-NARES.' Amazingly, this ship also became the victim of enemy attack ... but sadly, with rather more disastrous results.

This time, 77 children were drowned. Of those left, a total of 46 children managed to clamber aboard a lifeboat which then drifted in the storm-lashed North Atlantic. Their appalling ordeal lasted for eight days, during which time thirst and cold would be the worst trials of all. Initially, the lifeboat would contain a supply of water, condensed milk and ship-biscuits. Their daily 'menu' would probably have been a sip of water, a couple of spoonfuls of condensed milk and a ship-biscuit while supplies held out.

With heavy seas, persistent rain and cold, and water often rising to the level of the gunwales when the children would have to help in bailing out the overflowing water, it must have been a horrendous ordeal for any human being, far less a group of young children.

The story goes that to keep up their spirits, there were frequent games of 'I SPY', community singing of favourite songs and at one point, some of the boys joked about the possibility of their getting kilts this time, should they be lucky enough to land safely - yet again - in 'Bonnie Scotland'.

It must have been with a sense of deja-vu that the 46 young survivors were again brought safely back to the Clyde or 'The North British Port', as the newspapers would report. And no sooner were they ashore than the news of the boys' ambitions to wear the kilt somehow reached those in authority at Glasgow Corporation. In a very human gesture, it was speedily arranged that the brave young survivors should be fitted out not just with kilts, but with the whole bit of Highland regalia ... right down to sporrans, silver buckles, Glengarries and all. Later on, after a photograph-session, they were further treated to a visit to Glasgow's City Chambers, where they had tea with the then Lord Provost, Patrick Dollan.

The trauma of wartime evacuation of school-children affected all concerned. But surely the unluckiest evacuees of all were those ill-starred youngsters, who, having survived one submarine attack, later died when their second evacuee ship the 'CITY OF BENARES' went down, again due to enemy action.

More than half a century later, while I still cannot regard my own wartime evacuation through anything even remotely resembling rose-coloured spectacles, nevertheless I do realise and fully appreciate just how extremely lucky 'ma wee bree' and I myself were.

All we had to cope with were some rather self-important 'high heid yins' whose tiny bit of power as Billeting Officers had gone to their heads.

Thanks to enemy action and the vagaries of Fate, the 77 children who went down to a watery grave in the 'CITY OF BENARES' were not so fortunate.

SATURDAY MATINEE

Yet another cornerstone of our life in the Glasgow of the Thirties was the cinema, or 'ra picturs' as we Glesga weans were wont to call it. And as an essential and highly enjoyable part of our growing-up, many a local 'flea-pit' we patronised.

Saturday matinees were the most favoured performances, when for the princely sum of tuppence, we could enter not only the plush upholstered world of fantasy, but also the eminently desirable dream-state of Hollywood. But before reaching the comforting dark anonymity of whichever 'flea-pit' we had chosen on any particular day, there was first of all the agony of decision in allocating that last remaining penny of pocket-money. Each Friday night, Daddy would hand over my silver threepenny-piece and from that very moment, it would be a time of nail-biting indecision.

Certainly tuppence would already be spoken-for as my admittance fee for my weekly dose of Hollywood. But then would come the crunch... should I spend a halfpenny on two Highland Cream Toffees; ogo-pogo eyes which had the added attraction of changing colour; or would it be a Barrett's Sherbet Dab with its licquorice-tube for sooking-up the delicious powder and its supply of little 'cakes' of some indeterminate substance? Or should I go in for a spot of healthy eating with a couple of tangerines to eat during the show? This was always a tempting alternative, given that the tangerines had the added attraction of the pips which could be used as ammunition against sworn-enemies, over-officious usherettes or even some of the unsuspecting, but fully engrossed, young lovers in the back row?

Or should I deny myself that pleasure and hold on to my penny with a view to splurging the lot on either a poke of chips for a halfpenny, followed by a soda-stream bottle of pop with its little glass-marble holder? Or, why not go up-market and order a couple of delicious fritters coated in batter and fried in deep fat? These cost a farthing each, so were within my budget. Decisions! Decisions!

And on those rare occasions when I thought I'd be able to

27

scrounge some sweeties from my wee bree, Telfie, I'd keep my remaining pocket-money a prisoner until such time as I could blow the lot on a glorious half-hour of riotous living.... a visit to the local 'Tally-Wally' where one could sit in state at a bench-table and for the price of a penny, get a saucer-full of mushy peas soaked in vinegar,.. a real gourmet-treat.

As for the 'flea-pits' themselves, with their glamorous posters of beautiful film-stars; basket-work sofas in the foyer; scent-machines in the toilets; plush upholstered seats; and the perfumed disinfectant sprays shot out at regular intervals by the ornately-dressed usherettes, the whole scenario was a wonderland for children of our generation and of our social circumstances. Having said all that, it must also be stated that despite the sprays of  disinfectant, the 'flea-pits' were well named! And there was never a visit but what I brought home a souvenir of at least one highly athletic flea! Makes me itchy even to think of it!

But such inconvenience was a small price to pay for a few hours of splendid entertainment at a children's cinema matinee. Less fortunate were the seventy children who perished in the Paisley cinema disaster at the Hogmanay matinee on the last Tuesday of 1929. This happened at the 'GLEN' cinema when about 700 children had crushed into the hall to watch a double-feature, 'THE CROWD' and a cowboy-film entitled 'DESPERADO DUDE.' At one point there had been smoke issuing in one section of the hall and, although unknown to the children in the audience, the danger was soon over, nevertheless, the children started a stampede. Close on fifty children were severely injured, while the seventy young victims were later interred in a mass burial at Hawkhead Cemetery.

In 1929, I myself was only one year old and so, of course, had no way of knowing first-hand of this terrible tragedy. But over the years of my growing-up, especially when I was old enough to be left in charge of Telfie, each Saturday, before releasing us, Mammy would re-iterate the tale of the cinema disaster in nearby Paisley and then go on to instruct me to be extra-careful of my precious charge. She would tell me again and again to keep Telfie by my side at all times. This was easier said than done, given my wee bree's liking for wandering-off and for getting up to high jinks with the drinking-fountain in the men's toilet. Most times over the years, I did manage to obey Mammy's instructions to the letter. But there was one memorable occasion when things very nearly came unstuck. It happened like this...

MY DARKEST HOUR

I t was the last afternoon of our holiday and Telfie had been promised a treat for having been "A good boy." My mouth tightened in disgust as I thought over his record of behaviour during the past fortnight. Apart from having crashed through my precious master-piece for the sand-castle competition; caused a near-riot in the Museum; created havoc at the Children's Corner, and polluted and bespoiled the waters of the Moat, his behaviour had more or less followed its usual pattern. And no matter what the disaster, what crisis he had initiated, still the blond curls and twinkling blue eyes had come bobbing and smiling through, leaving behind a trail of desolation and a posse of devoted admirers.

With the cloudburst at Noon, our plans for a picnic had been shelved; and with the signs of a different type of cloudburst written large on Telfie's face, Mammy had rushed to say;
"Never mind, my wee darling. Jenny'll take you to the pictures. You'd like that, son. Now wouldn't you?"

Whether or not I would be equally delighted, nobody bothered to ask!

Mammy went on;
"You've been such a good wee laddie, Telfie. It'll be a real nice treat for you. Who wants a rotten old picnic when you can go to the pictures instead. And I'll give Jenny money for to buy ye a wee sweet-bite."

This was followed by angelic smiles from Telfie, pursed lips and eyes raised to Heaven by me, and reams of instructions from Mammy. She emphasised that I should keep Telfie by the hand at all times, but especially when passing the fountains and the Bathing Station and when walking along the Promenade; should not let him to the lavatory unattended; should not let him eat any rubbishy sweeties, it was to be a stick of barley sugar or nothing; should not give him any of the bags of stale, broken biscuits which he loved and would be sure to demand as ransom to ensure his good behaviour; should keep a watchful eye and a rag ready for his runny nose; and finally should take him to the "Palace" rather than the other wee picture house up the High Street. This last instruction was accompanied by an admonitory finger.

"Mind now, Jenny! The picture at yon other place is not suitable for the wee darlin'. It's a lovely film at the "Palace". Telfie will jist love seeing yon wee dwarfs. And clever wee laddie that he is, he can sing their song already, so he can. Can't you, my wee pet?"

The wee pet could. And did! He heigh-ho, heigh-hoed his way down Ardmory Road, past the Thomson Fountain, past the Bathing Station, and all along the Promenade, much to my disgust and to the amusement of passers-by. He heigh-ho, heigh-hoed with gusto, with bravado, with disregard for the proper words and with a total lack of tune. All the while, his fat little curls danced across his unfurrowed brow and his too-long kilt went swinging and swirling with the movement of his body.

I tugged again at his hand.

"Telfie! Will you shut yer face! Jist shut yer cake-hole! Put a padlock on yer geggie! Bung a sock in it. Dae what ye like. But just SHUT UP!"

Telfie's only reply was to launch into yet another verse of his own composition. I tried again.

"Telfie! I'm sick fed up with listenin' to ye. Ye might be a daft wee midget, I'll grant ye that. But ye're no' one of yon wee dwarfs. And I'll tell ye somethin' else, china. I'm NOT your bloody Snow-White."

He stopped dead in his tracks. Then, peering up at me through his halo of sausage-curls, he whimpered;

"YOU a BAD girl, Jenny! You said a bad word! Me tell Mammy! You said BLOOD.......

A slap to his bare legs brought tears to Telfie, disapproving stares from other holiday-makers and a moment of complete and utter joy to me.

The big picture was just about to start as we followed the usherette and her torch to our seats. Not one person stood up to let us past and we were left to fight our way as best we could. We squeezed past

31

the line of knees, trampled over the battalion of toes and fought for every inch of space. The cries and curses of the down-trodden followed us and rang in our ears. We had almost reached our seats when there was yet another yelp of pain as Telfie, game to the last, stood on one final foot. With a muttered, 'Sorry Mister', we at last reached the haven of our seats and sank into the comfort of the rich red plush upholstery.

I folded my arms across my chest, stretched out my feet to the ridge of the seat in front of me and prepared to leap on to my trusty steed and gallop off to adventure. I was deep in the wilds of the untamed West, when as though from a great distance, I heard;

"Ah'm too warm."

I kept my eyes on the screen, my body on the horse, and in the best cinema tradition, muttered out of the side of my mouth;

"Well, take your coat off! Daft wee puddin' that ye are!"

Telfie needed no second bidding. He jumped down from the seat, which at once snapped back with a noise more fearsome than any so far produced from the Lone Ranger's gun. There seemed to be some sort of struggle going on, both on the screen and off. At length, I was forced to ask;

"For heaven's sake, Telfie! What's wrong now?"

A tearful voice said;

"Ah'm stuck!"

With a sigh, I dragged my eyes away from the screen, leapt from my horse and sauntered over to the rescue.

The sight that met my eyes gave me a fit of the giggles. Poor wee Telfie! He was stuck and no mistake. In fact, he now wore his coat like a strait-jacket and the more he struggled, the more firmly enmeshed he became. The sound of my laughter rose, the tears streamed down my face and my giggles were now beyond control. It was at this point that a hand from the patron in the seat behind, tapped me on the shoulder. Beer-fumes wafted over me, as a disembodied voice said,

"Listen, hen! Ah've paid guid dole money for tae come into this flea-pit. And it's the Lone Ranger Ah'm wantin' tae hear. No' some daft wee gym-slip o' a lassie gigglin' her stupid heid aff. Get ra picture, hen?"

I blushed and nodded. Then once more in control, I leant across and tried to extricate Telfie from his coat. I struggled, pulled and then with one final effort, I managed to free him. That done, I shoved the bundle into his arms and plonked him back down on the seat. Just at that moment, a woman in a Robin Hood had sat down in the seat in front of his. Again, he wriggled about and twisted first one way, then the other. At last in desperation, he tugged at my sleeve and said,

"Jenny! Ah cannae see. My eyes is going all skelly with that big feather."

I dunted him with my elbow,

"SHUT UP! For heaven's sake, Telfie. You'll get us chucked oot. And then you'll no' see nothing at all!"

This was threat enough to make him sit still. And he did. He behaved. He sat like a statue for all of one minute. Then it started again. I did my best to ignore his antics and tried to catch up with the picture and my own particular project. Determined to form the biggest bubble ever seen with my bubble-gum, I was on the verge of success when Telfie pushed against me with his next complaint.

I turned to face him and dealt him another blow from my elbow. This caused him to jerk away but not before another disaster had befallen him. When I realised what had happened, I let out a yell;

"Wait till Mammy sees that! She'll murder me!"

Right on cue, came the reply from behind me,

"Murder ye? There's nae fear o that, hen! Ah'll get there first. I'll be happy to dae the dirty deed for her. Aye, it'll be a pleasure."

"Ah'm sorry, mister. It's my wee brother! You see, he's got bubble-gum stuck all over his hair!"

The beer-laden breath came closer and in a voice pitched low, yet with every syllable clear, said,

"Listen, sweetheart! It doesn't matter a tuppenny damn to me if the wee brat's got the Crown Jewels stuck on his heid, his face or ony other part o' his stinking body! All Ah'm interested in is seeing the damned picture in peace."

Telfie wriggled lower in his seat and started to cry. He tried to weep quietly and as usual, what came out were great, gulping, choking sobs. Up there on the screen, the Lone Ranger was overcoming impossible odds, but not even he could remove that feather. The weeping grew louder, behind us the screen enthusiast muttered curses and dire threats, while Robin Hood turned round from time to time to throw us a dirty look and another toss of that feather.

After much manoeuvring, I withdrew from my knicker-pocket a crumpled paper bag. The rustle of the paper alone was enough to make Telfie stop crying. Without a word, his hand shot forward into the darkness. When nothing was immediately forthcoming and his up-turned palm was still empty, he started again.

As the sobs gained in volume and it seemed that he was on course for one of his special marathon bouts, which normally ended in a screaming temper-tantrum complete with the banging of his little feet, I decided on desperate measures. I took the mass of toffee balls and banged it against the ash-tray which was clipped to the seat in front of me. Nothing happened. At least not to the toffee balls. But the noise stirred Robin Hood into further action.

She rose from her seat, tramped over the line of toes and approached the usherette. In the ensuing commotion, Telfie and I made good our escape. At first, the novelty of being in the back seat, where there seemed to be more action going on than there was on the screen, kept Telfie interested and quiet. Not only that, but I permitted him to sit on the upturned seat for a better view of proceedings. All this while, I had been trying to tear the toffee balls apart with my bare hands. At last, I shoved the sticky mess into Telfie's hand with the words,

"It's too tough to break. Just you suck it, son."

He did. Right through the big picture he sucked. All the way through the news, he sucked. On past the trailers for the following week's films, he sucked. He sucked with appreciation, with relish, with noise, as he devoured the toffee, savoured it and trickled its sweetness through his teeth.

The tangerine was, if anything, an even greater success than the toffee balls. It had the added attraction of the pips. These he spat out like bullets all through the first half of the second feature.

I had even let Telfie go unattended to the lavatory and apart from coming back with his trousers at half-mast, everything seemed to be all right. My worries were over. With a sigh of relief, I climbed back on to the mortuary slab with the crazed girl who was struggling against the bonds which held her. The Terror of the Waxworks was crouched low, as with fangs bared and hypodermic in hand, he snarled at his victims. Suddenly, his voice changed. I could have sworn I heard him say,

"Ah want ma Mammy!"

Lightning flashed, thunder rolled, the girls shrieked for mercy, but nothing would stop the Beast and that hypodermic. He roared like one demented, as with arm poised over them, he prepared to strike. Into this cacophony, a voice said,

"Jenny! Ah don't like it! Don't want to see it. I'm scared. Ah'm feart o that big monstra. Don't want to watch."

With a flash of inspiration, I draped Telfie's coat over his bubble-gum pink curls.

"There! Is that better, son?"

For a while, there was silence. The Human Beast renewed his attack. He was descending to depths of unspeakable degradation, when right beside me, there was a strangled cry. I nearly jumped out of my skin. When I could trust myself to speak, I whispered,

"Sh! Wheesht, Telfie! It's nearly finished, son."

Telfie's reply was a choking sob, which far out-staged any sound as yet heard from the damsels in distress. The poor girls were still chained in their nightmare situation, but from the sounds coming from under that draped coat, their plight was as nothing compared to that of poor wee Telfie.

It was then I realised! There was drama going on right there beside me, and an even greater trauma than that being enacted on the screen.

No thunder rolled, no lightning flashed, no monster terrorised and no victim screamed. Yet, the horror was there. It was all there in that guttural sound still coming from Telfie. It was with a sinking of the heart and a feeling of doom that I heard him gasp out from the depths of the coat which still covered his head,

"Jenny! Ah've SWALLOWED A BUTTON!"

In that moment, I realised that boats were not the only things to go adrift in Rothesay. Somewhere deep inside wee Telfie's fat belly, a button had joined the other delicacies and was even now, sloshing around in a sea of stale biscuits, lemonade, sugar, syrup and tangerine.

The holidays, events, accidents, and general trauma of Telfie's upbringing can and do fill an entire book on their own. Sufficient for "TALES of a GLASGOW CHILDHOOD" to state that, miraculous as it may seem, we both survived the ordeal! And lived to tell the tales, each in our own way.

In adult life, we became the best of friends and I took to calling my brother by his "Sunday" name. Somehow, "Wee Telfie" no longer suited the bearded, dignified and august personage who was by then the Headmaster of a world-renowned boarding-school in Canada. From then on, it was "Hugh." And Wee Telfie, his golden curls, his winning ways, and his temper-tantrums faded into the mists of Time.

GRANNY McGUINNESS
- QUEEN O' RA CLOSE

Throughout Scotland in the tight-knit community of tenement life, and especially in the 1920/30's era, every neighbour residing up a child's close was almost like a member of the family.

And as far as these adults went, they had the same proprietorial rights as yer Maw and Paw... they were fully entitled to gie ye a 'guid belt aroon the ear-hole' if ever you were daft enough, or daring enough, to be cheeky or to step out of line in any socially unacceptable way.

As far as I was concerned, there was one particular neighbour who fully exercised her rights in shaping my personality in the way it should go, and that was auld Granny McGuinness. She too lived in a single-end like ours, just across the ground-floor landing from us, and from such a position, she monitored my every single move and almost - or so it seemed to me - each living breath I took!

Like my own Granny Brigton, Granny McGuinness had come from Ireland as a young bride, when she and her husband were in search of work. After a horrendous crossing over the Irish Sea when, having paid their sixpence per skull steerage-passenger fare, they were herded in like animals and had stood shoulder-to-shoulder throughout the entire nightmare voyage.

Once safely arrived in Glasgow, they discovered to their horror that the City of their dreams, where they had hoped to make a living, if perhaps not exactly a fortune, was already saturated with desperate, poverty-stricken unemployed immigrants. And apart from the Irish immigrants, there were also hordes of equally miserable people who had been evicted from the ruined crofts of the Scottish Highlands. And to make matters worse, factories and other assorted workplaces were littered with crudely-printed notices which announced in no uncertain terms that 'NO IRISH NEED APPLY.'

Not that the ogress Granny McGuinness ever discussed any of her business or her past history with me, but as a child, I often overheard long, intense discussions with Mammy, as the two women, despite the age-gap, confided in each other their hopes, dreams and fears over a pot of Granny's famous stewed 'tay.' Then, in later life, my curiosity still aroused, I was able to fill in the gaps and round out Granny's particular story.

It appeared that the cancer of unemployment had entered the soul of her once-industrious and hopeful husband, Patrick to such an extent that eventually Granny - whose first name I did eventually discover to be Abigail - became the main-stay of the family, with Patrick something of a professional layabout.

Between carrying and rearing nine children, Granny took in washing; washed the stairs and landings of posh 'wally-tiled' closes; sold treacle-toffee, candytuft and toffee-balls out of her front window; and even at one point, worked in a rag-store. This last occupation was always referred to sotto voce - not that Granny was in any way ashamed of a good honest day's work,- but it seemed that her employer, the owner of the rag-store, had been a 'lecherous auld man.'

As a child, I never did discover exactly what this was, nor even what such a description entailed. However, I did gather that as far as the employment of the then beauteous young Irish bride, being in close quarters with a 'lecherous auld man' was something of no value or interest and indeed, something to be avoided at all costs. This dawned on me the day that I heard the old woman tell Mammy;

"Ah jist tellt the auld b----- that any gropin' tae be done would be done by me in pickin' through yon mountains o' flea-bitten rags. And if he'd any ither ideas, then as a fugitive frae the slums o' Dublin, Ah could well fend for masell. Forbye, ma man, Patrick, was a devil in drink and he'd be happy for tae belt him wan an' a'. Aye, Patrick wid soon settle the hash o' ony lecherous auld beast."

Granny's conversation always tended to be a strange mixture of Glesga patter and the softer strains of auld Ireland. However, on the many occasions she had to reprimand me, she invariably sounded like a grand-dame from a wally-close in the City's West End! Whether or not this was a conspiracy between Mammy and her guid neebor, I never did discover. However, it was highly likely that Mammy had indeed divulged to the older woman, her dream of having her weans learn tae speak 'posh', and so perhaps this was Granny's way of furthering my education!

As I recall it now, some sixty years later, the main 'causus-belli' between Granny and me was my lack of proper respect for the twin gods of her pipe-clayed doorstep, and her gleaming brass door furnishings... and of course, let us not forget that other mainstay - her near-idolatry of my golden-haired, curly-headed wee bree, Telfie. Many a tale I could tell about that.

But for the moment, to return to Granny and her many peccadilloes, she was a martyr to cleanliness. Alone now in old age, with her sainted Patrick in the Land o' the Leal and her large family scattered to the four corners of the earth, Granny devoted her life, her energies, and her gnarled arthritic limbs to scrubbing, polishing and dusting every inch of her single-end wee palace, even to the very bounds of her territorial rights at the close-mouth.

Never a day went by but what Granny polished her letter-box, bell-pull knob, and brass lion's head. I can see her yet - in long skirt, sack-cloth apron and baggy, stretched cardigan, whose sleeves did double-duty as a convenient handkerchief, she polished those brasses with a red velvet pad, and with such vigour, it was as if her life depended on it.

Out of sheer devilment and greatly daring, I used to creep across the landing and then with bated breath, press sticky fingers to Granny's letter-box. This was always a great thrill to me, especially since its gleaming facade was normally unsullied, on account of the fact that to the best of my knowledge, Granny had only ever received one letter! And even on that truly memorable occasion, such was Granny's reputation, that the Postie had had the good sense to knock on the door itself, rather than either pull the bell or bespoil the glowing brilliance of the hallowed letter-box!

Granny must have had an inbuilt radar system, for all too often, she would open the door in one quick, dramatic movement, catch me red-handed in the dastardly deed and yank me inside, ben her hoose, there to give me a skelpit lethering on my bahoochie and/or a lecture on good behaviour, invariably delivered in Granny's best 'pan-loaf' voice.

Perhaps I wasn't quite as daring as I liked to think, for I never once had the courage to bespoil either Granny's treasured coconut-fibre mat at her door or her bewhorled pattern of pipeclay artistry surrounding it. I left such outrageous behaviour to the 'heavy mob' - such scum as Durty Dick from the next close or Saft Sandy from the top floor.

Poor Saft Sandy, mentally he wisnae quite the full twenty shullins in the pound, and for the reward of a liquorice pipe, he would do anybody's bidding.

Like that time he was instructed to scoop up a shovelful of dog's dirt and deposit it on Granny's fibre door-mat. Deeply intent on obeying orders, Saft Sandy didn't hear Granny's approach until it was too late. But what did surprise me on that occasion, Sandy got neither belt across the ear-lug, nor skelpit letherin' on his bum, such as would have been my reward, even for a much lesser crime. Instead, a glowering Granny merely took him by the hand and marched the somewhat bemused Sandy up four flights of stairs to his own home. From there, she engaged in a guid-gaun' 'sterr-heid brawl' with Sandy's long-suffering Mammy, who at one stage of the proceedings pointed out that she did not see what all the fuss was about - surely all Granny had to do was to administer a well-aimed slap at Sandy's ample behind?

Enjoying this battle of words to the full, I had crept up a couple of flights, so as not to miss a single word. Thus I was in time to hear Granny say,

"Me belt pair wee Sandy? It's that whit ye're seyin'? Naw, naw, lassie! Sandy is wan o' God's protected craiturs. The pair wee laddie hasnae got a' his marbles, God help him! So, all Ah'm sayin' tae ye, Meestress Simpson is this - jist you try for tae keep him awa' frae yon Durty Dick, for he's a bad influence."

At this, I could hear the murmur of agreement from Sandy's Mammy, but before she could say anything further, Granny went on;

"Aye, Meestress Simpson, while ye're at it, giein' Durty Dick an ear-bashin', ye kin grab a haud o' him and wheech him roon here for tae clean up yon stinkin' mess on ma guid doormat!"

And, at least as far as Granny was concerned, that was the matter resolved. But there was a sequel - and a somewhat surprising one at that - I often afterwards caught a glimpse of Granny sneaking a newly-baked potato-cake dripping with butter out to Saft Sandy as he played in the filth and amid the rusting rubbish of the back-court middens. And how the face of the poor deranged lad would light up at the sight of his new friend, a gift-laden Granny McGuinness - especially on those occasions when the kind-hearted and lonely old woman went the extra mile and provided him with a steaming chunk of her famous and delicious 'clootie-dumplin'.

Yes! I learnt a lot from my guid neebor, Granny McGuinness... good behaviour, polite speech, respect for the needs of others less fortunate, whether in health, estate or mental well-being. But above all, I learnt compassion.

And as I said at the beginning of this article, in the tight-knit community of tenement life, every neighbour up a child's close was almost like a member of the family.

In the case of Granny McGuinness, old, crippled and abandoned by her own kith and kin, the extended family of the close was her lifeline to sanity. It gave her hope, enjoyment and a very real purpose in her old-age.

Is it any wonder that she was known - sometimes in awe or in fear - but more often in affection, as Granny McGuinness, 'Ra QUEEN O' RA CLOSE.'

LEERIE, LEERIE, LIGHT THE LAMPS

As Mammy and I came out of the City Bakeries, leaving its warmth and comfortable smells behind us, it was starting to get dark and the raw winter night was already closing in. Laden as we were with stringed cake-boxes dangling from every finger, it was all I could do to keep up with Mammy who seemed determined to rush on ahead. As yet, the street lamps had not been lit. Even worse, I was finding it difficult to keep my precious cargo safe, especially as the string became more and more entangled and the boxes bounced off one another with every step I took. Suddenly I had an idea and called out;

"Mammy! Look, Mammy! Therr's Leerie."

As I had hoped she would, Mammy stopped in her tracks and peered into the gathering dusk.

"Aye, so it is, wee yin. My an' yer gey gleg in the e'en, Jenny. Ah must be feedin' ye ower many o' thon raw carrots."

I giggled, all the while taking full advantage of the respite from our route march to ease the string out of their beds of my flesh. Mammy transferred some of her own packages, then cupped her free hand and shouted;

"Hello therr, Leerie. Whit's up the nicht? Ye're awfy late, so ye urr."

At her words, the man stopped with pole in mid-flight. He gave us a cheery wave. Next, he opened the glass cover of the lamp standard, inserted the pole and at once the gas flickered into life. That done, he walked to the kerb, paused to let a Drummond's coal horse and cart trundle past, then shambled over the cobble-stones to join us. He doffed his bunnet.

"Evenin' tae ye, Mrs. McCracken." Then looking down at me, festooned with packages as I was, he chucked me under the chin and stated the obvious,

"Hello wee yin. This you helpin' yer Mammy for the nicht?" I took a step back, but made no reply. He tried again.

"Hoo's yersell, Jenny? Urr ye aff the schule the noo? Wi' ra holidays an' a' that?"

When there was still no reply, Mammy frowned at me and with head cocked on one side, gave a barely perceptible nod. Right on cue and in the biggest bool-in-the-mooth voice I could muster, I said,

"Aih'm very well, thenk you, Mister Ferguson. And yes, thenk you very much for asking, Aih'm enjoying to the full my Christmas holidays from Greenfield."

There was a moment's stunned silence before he recovered sufficiently to say,

"Aye, weel, uhu! That's rerr, hen, so it is. Aye, Ah'm awfy gled for tae hear that."

Then turning to Mammy, the wee bauchle said,

"And whit aboot yon wee angel o' a Telfie, Mrs McCracken? Is he no' aboot reddy for tae enter the sacred halls o' learnin' forbye?"

Mammy laughed in obvious delight that Leerie too was a member of Telfie's devoted band of admirers.

"Weel, Telfie's a wee while for tae go yet, Fergie. But, uch, the wee darlin', Ah'll be in nae hurry for tae see him marchin' awa' wi' a school-bag and a playpiece. Ah don't mind tellin' ye."

They laughed together and the lamplighter said,

"Weel, playpiece or nae sweet-bite, Missus, therr's wan thing for certain sure. Thae weans o' yours is gettin' the best. The richt kinna feedin'. God alone kens how ye dae it, Missus."

Mammy did not answer at once. Then she sighed,

"Weel, Ah'll say this, Leerie. It's no' easy."

He laid a hand on Mammy's arm.

"Easy or no', it's worth it, hen. Ye kin tak ma word for that. Aye, that's the God's honest truth. Worth it!"

I could feel the man staring at me, and on meeting his eyes, I was aware of a bleakness in their depths as he said,

"Aye, Jenny, ye're a richt lucky wee wean, so ye urr. YOU'RE no the wan wi' rickets."

I was surprised to see that Mammy was blinking back a tear and she had to clear her throat a couple of times before she again spoke and even I could tell that she was deliberately trying to change the subject.

"Ah wis jist saying, Leerie, that ye wis awfy late the nicht. Wis therr sumthin' up? Whitever's happened, ye'll huv upset Granny McGuinness, for the auld biddie aye sets her guid clock by ye."

The lamplighter opened his mouth to reply, but catching sight of my eyes eager for the latest bit of Govan news, he first jerked a thumb in my direction. Catching his meaning, Mammy at once said,

"Jenny! Awa' an' play ower at the tram stop for a meenit."

As always on the pavement around the tramcar stop, there were a number of brightly coloured tickets lying in the gutter and I skipped away quite happily, meaning to gather up a handful to add to my existing collection at home. However, I had reckoned without the burden of my cake-boxes, and no matter how I tried, I just could not grasp even a few of the treasures so near and yet so far. With a tut of annoyance, I realised that I'd have to leave the tickets for another time. However, as I stood there toeing patterns in a puddle, I heard snatches of the whispered conversation still going on a few feet away from me.

There was a gasp from Mammy and this was followed by a phrase spoken with greater volume and emphasis than what had previously been said;

"Aye, it's true, Missus. His face was like a pun o' raw mince! An' ye should huv saw the ither fella! God almichty, Ah've saw many a stramash here in ra streets o' Govan. But nivver nuchin' like whit Ah've saw this nicht. A bloody battle, so it wis. An the fella wi' the minced face, he wis still goin' berserk wi' a razor. That wis afore Ah got tae him, like! Ah don't mind tellin' ye, Missus, ma herrt wis goin' like the clappers, so it wis. But somebody had tae stop the daft gowk afore he murdered the ither drunk."

Again that intake of breath from Mammy. I edged nearer and above my head could just make out from their lowered tones something about razors and gang-fights outside a pub round in Govan Road. Suddenly Mammy caught sight of my upturned face. She glanced at Leerie and with a finger to her lips, then said, "Weel, Leerie, Ah'd better get awa' and let ye get oan wi' yer guid work. And mind noo, if Ah don't see ye till next year, a' ra best. If onybody deserves a bit o' guid luck, it's yersell. Especially after whit you've did this nicht. Ye're a hero, Leerie. Aye, a hero, an' Ah'll be tellin' a' ra neebors whit a brave man ye urr, so Ah wull. Weel, cheerio, an' a' ra best.

Ye're a man in a million."

As we left Leerie in some confusion at the praise which had been heaped on his bald head, I made as if to continue along Langlands Road. However, Mammy with a jerk of her hand indicated that we were instead going around the corner. She smiled at me and said,

"Ah've jist decided, hen. We'll go intae the Chippy's in Elder Street and get a wee treat for tae tak hame. A wee bag o' fritters, eh no?"

The very word gave a lift to my heart, a lightness to my step and I almost ran to the door of the chip shop. The vinegar-laden blast of heat met me at the doorway and drew me into its comforting warmth inside the shop. As I stood, threepenny bit in hand, the delicious smells wafted over me as I waited impatiently to be served. Then, as my seasoned, vinegared order was scooped into the bag, it was all I could do to refrain from stretching across the counter to sample a piece of the golden delicacy. Once out in the street again, we walked past the Church on the Steamie corner. As always, I raised my head to practice my reading in trying to decipher the week's inspirational message on the Bible poster. But this time, the sight that met my eyes gave me a fit of the giggles. Attached to the corner of the board was a rusting, battered and stinking old chamber pot.

Tears of laughter were streaming down my face and I was on the point of spelling out the long words of the Bible message when a slap to my right leg brought me to my senses. "That's quite enough of that, my lady! Some drink-crazed eejit must have thought he was being smart. But therr's nae call for you tae go' oan like a half-wit as weel. So, jist knock it aff, Jenny."

At once suitably chastened and with the promise of those fritters, the smell of which was already goin' roon ma herrt like a hairy worm, I continued the rest of the way in silence. Arrived at our close-mouth, Mammy put out a hand and said, "Jenny! A quick word afore we go in. Ye were gey rude tae Leerie back therr awhiles. At first, no' answering him when he spoke that civil tae ye; and then speakin' tae him as if ye wis the Lady Muck hersell. An' him, pair wee lamplighter that he is, being that nice tae ye. Wid ye mind jist tellin' me? Jist whit was a' that daft cantrip aboot, eh?"

"Uch, Mammy! It's thon song. The big boys at schule sing it, so they dae. Ah don't really know it. Something aboot.... 'Leerie, Leer-ie, licht the lamps wi' yer skinny legs and crooked shanks.' It was jist, weel, Ah didnae want ony o' thae big boys for tae see me talking tae....."

A well-aimed slap finished the sentence for me.

"Ya stupit wee scunner that ye urr! Don't you ever say or even think such a thing ivver again. Dae ye hear me? Leerie's a richt decent wee man, so he is. A real kenspeckle figure daein' a grand job here in Govan. Helpin' tae keep wur streets safe. And for whit he's did ra nicht, he should be gettin' a medal, instead o' a lot o' snash frae a wee bitch like you. It's no' his fault he's got rickets and hasnae had a' your advantages. Advantages! Hmph! Jist wasted oan a wee brat like you, so they are. Jist pure wasted."

Another slap and a hearty shove sent me hurtling through the close. Arrived at our own door, Mammy turned to me and said,

"And ye kin stop a' that snivelling. At wanst, Madam! And jist you awa' in and collect the wee darlin' frae Granny McGuinness. Ah'll get in ben the hoose, steer up ra fire and get ra kettle oan."

Suitably chastened, but with the promise of greater things to come, I stepped smartly across to Granny's door. About to give a tattoo with the brass door-knocker, I turned when I again heard Mammy's voice,

"And Jenny! Therr's wan thing mair. Ye kin jist forget a' aboot eatin' ony fritters the nicht. Wee Telfie'll get a double helping, so he wull. Mibbe that wull learn ye for tae mind yer P's and Q's when ye're talking tae folk. Noo! Awa' wi' ye! Hurry up and get a haud o' the wean. The pair wee mite'll be fair stervin'. And as for ony idea o' yer steyin' up late the nicht... Weel, Ah'll huv tae see aboot that an' a'."

With a heart as heavy as the brass lion's head then clutched in my fingers, I knocked on Granny's door and awaited the next train of events.

I waited without hope, but secure in the certainty of gloom, family disaster and personal disappointment to follow in the few short hours still left of the year 1934.

HOGMANAY, 1934

In common with many O.A.P's, I find that I often look back and remember the "good old days", and not least when we approach another year's end. Throughout my life I've spent some memorable Hogmanies - in Glasgow's 'posh' West End; in inner-city Birmingham; in down-town Winnipeg; in Tenerife, the 'Island of Eternal Spring'; in Rothesay in the Madeira of Scotland; in the African Bush in the Northern Cameroons - you name it, I've been there, taking an active part and drinking not such a very wee 'deogh and doris.'

But the Hogmanay which wins hands down for fond memories was that first one in Glasgow's Govan when Mammy finally allowed me 'tae stey up fur ra bells.'

The year was 1934, and Depression or no Depression, Mammy was determined to give us all a real guid 'wee nicht.' So it was that 31st December found Mammy and I coming out of my favourite shop in Govan's Langlands Road. We were laden with bestringed cake-boxes dangling from every finger and it was already dark and the raw winter night seemed to seal us in, the moment we left the warmth and comfortable smells of the City Bakeries.

Later that same evening, after a frantic rush through gas-lit streets as we held our precious cargo aloft, all the while expertly dodging some richt wee nyaffs who had obviously started early on the serious business of Hogmanay imbibing, we were again safely home in our own cosy wee single-end.

And thanks to Mammy's efforts, oor wee palace was gleaming like new. On the mantelpiece, the brass candle sticks, set at equi-distant points from the 'wedding knock', shone and sparkled in the light from the polished-for-dear-life black range. The tea-caddy twinkled like gold and even those proud guardians of the mantelpiece - the guid wally-dugs - had had their annual bath. Over against the wall, the table covered with an altar-white cloth, was set with every delicacy one could imagine. There were plates of home-made 'pangcakes', triangles of shortbread, sponge fingers, wedges of Black Bun, slices of clootie dumplin'; boiled ham 'sangwiches', not to mention the City Bakeries 'specials' of pineapple tarts, 'Effel' towers and lovely Empire biscuits. As far as liquid refreshment went, there was a bottle of elderberry wine, a stone jar of ginger beer, a bottle of lemonade, more commonly called 'ginger' by Glesga weans; and a half-bottle of some amber fluid with the intriguing name of 'Teacher's.'

The first 'guest' to arrive was our friend, neighbour and terror of the local weans, Granny McGuinness. As Mammy and Daddy ushered her from the dank close into the warmth and spluttering gas-light of our single-end, we saw the crone in all her finery. Granny's normal garb, which she wore when scrubbing her doorstep free of dog's dirt, polishing her brasses or doing a spot of artistic design work with pipe-clay, was an ancient skirt, once black but grown green and limp with age; a coarse, stretched, knitted garment which had probably started life as a cardigan; and her 'badge of office', the sack-cloth apron which did double duty as polishing rag, cleaning cloth and convenient, if somewhat rough, handkerchief.

But tonight, Granny's outfit, bizarre though it was, declared her to be in every respect, 'Ra Queen o' Ra Close.' From the pink satin sheath which did its inadequate best to enclose her gargantuan bulk, to the ribbon of green curtain material wound somewhat inexpertly around her steel-skewered bun atop her head to the flea-ridden length of some indeterminate fur around her scraggy neck, Granny was indeed a jewel among women.

Having been duly congratulated on her annual sartorial transformation, Granny simpered and preened like a young girl. Then, still mightily pleased with herself, she took my wee bree, Telfie, up on her knee and pulled her chair 'into the ribs.' At once, Telfie, much to Mammy's consternation, put out a hand and stroked the flea-ridden fur which now trailed so negligently from Granny's neck. At this, Granny's face softened, she placed a tender, arthritic hand on Telfie's curly head, grinned at the company in general, over the graveyard of her teeth, and said,

"Uch, the wee darlin'. Did Granny pit oan her best claes fur yer pairty, son?"

More as a ploy to get Telfie away from the danger zone than

anything, Mammy quickly directed Granny's attention to the festive board. Granny creaked her old bones out of her chair. Then as her rheumy eyes took in the table, not in its usual garishly-patterned oil-cloth, but dressed overall in its virginal-white linen sheet, her eyes filled.

"Bejasus! Whit a spread! Ye've fair did us prood the nicht, Janet."

Mammy accepted the compliment as her due, gave a gracious nod and opened her mouth to speak. But Granny was too quick for her.

"Ah tell ye this, Janet. Ah huvnae saw a bean-feast like that since the black day Ah buried ma puir auld Patrick in the Sainted Isle."

Having delivered herself of this speech, Granny withdrew a rag from some inner region of her party frock and proceeded to weep noisily, much to the interest of us weans. At this, Mammy and Daddy exchanged glances. While Mammy then raised her eyes to heaven, Daddy rushed on to say,

"The day ye buried yer guid man, eh? Weel, that's as may be, Granny. But the nicht we're hopin' things'll be a damn sicht cheerier than a funeral tea!"

As it approached the witching hour, poor Daddy, being dark-haired, was bundled out into the freezing close, there to await the official signal of the birth of a New Year.

Meanwhile, Mammy slammed the door shut and then surveyed her home with a housewifely eye. She re-aligned the already soldier-straight display of plates, dichted the lid of an already spotlessly clean coal-bunker with the edge of her pinny. Then, for one hilarious moment, I thought she was about to dust, tidy-up, or in some way re-arrange the disaster that was Granny! However, the moment passed and Granny unaware of what danger she had been in, quite happily toasted her ample knees at the fire. We strained to hear the promised Hogmanay bells and hooters, but as yet, all that could be heard was the dripping of the goose-neck tap, the crackle of the coals and the metallic ticking of the clock as it counted off the last minutes of the old year. Suddenly, our peace was shattered by a shriek from Mammy.

"For heaven's sake! Wid youse a' tak a gander at that! And here's me thinkin' Ah wis ready! Granny, ye've left a durty plate under yer chair!"

Mammy leapt to her feet, grabbed the plate and dashed over with it to the jaw-box. She rinsed it under the tap, gave it a quick dicht with a red-striped tea-towel and shoved it into the press. Just in time! At that very moment, a cacophony erupted... the ships' hooters echoed from the river; bells were ringing and windows were screeching as unseen hands prised open tenement windows to let out the old and usher in the glad New Year. From the close, there were riotous sounds of merry-making. Mammy ran to the door, threw it open wide and flung her arms around Daddy. The brave new Year of 1935, and whatever it held for the future, had begun.

Some hours later, the celebrations were in full swing. Those guests who were either sufficiently outgoing or just suitably anaesthetized, had already done their 'party-pieces.' Thus, we'd already had a rendition of Grandpa Mac's favourite poem 'Imphm! That awfy wurd Imphm.'; the Queen o' ra close had unbent sufficiently to screech her way through "Danny Boy", although from her frequent intervals to mop up her copious tears, it was clear that the 'Danny Boy' of her mental image went by the name of 'Me puir auld Patrick'; and Stoorie Sandy's monologue of 'An Emigrant's Fareweel tae his auld Granny' had taken us mile after weary mile through the far-flung wilds of Canada to the sad realisation that never again in this mortal life would he see his dear auld Granny in her wee but-and-ben which overlooked 'Sweet Rossy Bay.'

In the sudden silence that followed this harrowing tale, the only sound then to be heard was that of weeping as we each sympathised with the plight of that poor young emigrant laddie, far from family, Highland croft and his beloved Bonnie Scotland. Such a tale was enough to break the stoutest of hearts. The only person not visibly affected was Grandpa Mac.... mind you, given his great age, it must indeed have been many a long day since he had clapped eyes on his Granny!

Seeing the party spirit evaporate in much the same way as had 'Teacher's water of life,' Daddy at once stepped into the breach. Grabbing the empty 'ginger' bottle, he declared that 'for to give a wee bit o' encouragement to the backward-at-coming-forward members of our select group,' he would 'spin ra boattle.'

Wouldn't you just know it? On its first twirl, the boattle stopped at yours truly... and me, a real shrinking violet if ever there was one! In a near-panic, and already purple in the face with embarrassment, I was chewing at the skin on the inside of my cheek as I tried to decide on what form my 'turn' might take. Should I try for what I was already sure would be an inexpertly-executed Highland Fling or would it be better to attempt a half-remembered poem from Miss Murray's class when, despite that lady's accuracy with her trusty Lochgelly, she had nevertheless failed to instil into me any great love of poetry! Deciding to opt for the Muse as the lesser of two evils, I got to my feet. Then in an agony of embarrassment, I stood before my hushed and expectant audience, straightened with trembling hand the apron of my hand-me-doon kilt, cleared my throat and finally with hands clasped in the appropriate dramatic manner, I started on my recitation...

'Ah'm gonnae recite tae youse a wee poem cried, "A Faither Tae ye A" by the famous Govan poet, astronomer and Workhouse tailor, James Nicholson.

I had got as far as the first line;

'Oh whaes a' thae wee bairnies....

when I was saved, not by the bell, but by a burst of piping from the other side of the door.

My saviour turned out to be none other than my Uncle Erchie, re splendent in his jumble-sale kilt, tweed jacket, the pockets of which were carrying a bigger load of whisky and Eldorado than any Clyde-built vessel. He cut a dashing figure, although the effect was somewhat spoiled when a fitfully-dozing Telfie suddenly woke up and, finding him-self having an eyeball-to eyeball confrontation with some weird ani-mal, immediately set up a banshee

51

wailing, convinced that the 'monster' was about to devour him! It took all of Erchie's 'savoire-faire' as a sophisticated wee nyaff frae Govan to reassure Telfie that all was well. Even so, he was not fully convinced until Uncle Erchie prised open the animal's head and withdrew from his sporran a silver sixpence for 'A brave wee laddie.'

Another libation of 'Teacher's best' and again Erchie, confidence fully restored, tucked his bagpipes firmly under his left oxter and off he went again.

If you've ever heard a set of bagpipes played at full-belt in a single-end, then you need no words of mine to describe the racket! If on the other hand, you've been spared that life-threatening experience, why should I be the one to remove your rose-coloured specs? All I will say, is that the ear-splitting rendition of every Scottish air then known to man was played that memorable night by a somewhat inebriated Uncle Erchie...

JET AGE GRANDMOTHER

We met at a coffee morning.
"I'm a grandmother," she said,
her face aglow with the light
of love and pride and ownership...

Blue-rinsed hair, false eyelashes,
film-star make-up and red-slashed lips,
scarlet-tipped nails and slave bangles,
pendant earrings which whirled as she spoke
and enough gold chains
to adorn a team of visiting mayors...
Dragging my eyes from this Hollywood clone
I thought back sixty years
to my own grandmother
with her sack-cloth apron, mob-cap
and her shawl a haven
for grandchildren.
Was it my imagination perhaps?
Or did I hear my Glasgow Granny say
from some ghostly beyond;
"I'm a grandmother"
And in that well-loved face
there still glowed the light
of love and pride and ownership.

A DISTANT MEMORY

When I was young
in Glasgow during the dark days of Depression,
I could walk in any park with safety.
Could meander to school
splashing through puddles,
my only fear?
That of my teacher's Lochgelly belt
which would crash down on my hand
should I arrive after that last peal
of school bell.
On arrival home
I'd get another beltin'.
In this way I learnt a new word -
not punctuality
but obedience -
obedience for life.